Johnny's Decisions

by Jeff Felardo
Illustrated by Mentol

This book is meant to act as an introduction to economic ideas. This particular book focuses on the idea of tradeoffs.

Dedicated to Giuseppe, Carina, and Matt Florell.

ISBN-13: 978-1503212442

ISBN-10: 1503212440

http://www.freeeconhelp.com/p/economics-for-kids.html

***The park is so much fun!* Thought Johnny,**

But the park is not fun at all when it rains.

“Hmmm…. I will go to the park today!”

At the park, Johnny ran into his good friend Adam.

"Hi Johnny, my birthday is on Saturday and I am having a party. We are going swimming," said Adam. "Do you want to come?"

"Yes, that sounds like fun," replied Johnny.

"Great, let's go play on the swings," said Adam.

“Five minutes left,” announced Johnny’s dad. “then it’s time to go home.”

Johnny stopped to think about what he wanted to do for the last five minutes. There were swings, slides, and many other choices. This would be hard.

“We could race to the other side of the park,” Adam suggested.

“Yes, we could have a race to the other side of the park,

Or

we could climb up and go down the slide a lot of times in five minutes,” Johnny said.

Johnny and Adam thought hard about their choice.

“Hmmm… what shall we do?”

“We can run anywhere,” Adam finally said. “But I think we can go up and down the slide one hundred times if we start now.”

“Race you to the slide!” yelled Johnny as he ran towards the slide.

That night during dinner the phone rang.

"It's Taylor," said Johnny's dad. "Her birthday is this Saturday and she wants to invite you. Can you go?"

“Of course!” replied Johnny. Taylor was his best friend after all.

That night, when Johnny went to bed he remembered that he had already told Adam he would go to his party.

***If I go to Adam's party I will get to swim and Adam is a good friend, but Taylor will be sad*, thought Johnny.**

But, if I go to Taylor's party Adam will be sad. But Taylor has been my best friend forever.

I really want to go to Taylor's party

But I also want to go to Adam's party.

"This is a hard choice, what shall I do?" he whispered as he fell asleep.

The next day, during dinner, Johnny talked to his Mom and Dad about the problem.

“I said I would go to both and now I am not sure what to do.”

Bonjour!

“You’re right, that is a problem,” responded his mom. “Whose party are you going to go to?”

“I want to go to both,” said Johnny with a sad look on his face. “But I can’t go to both because they are at the same time.”

“I would like to go to Adam’s party so I can go swimming.”

“Then you can’t go to Taylor’s party,” replied his mom.

***Hmmm... I can only go to one party, what shall I do?* Thought Johnny as he hung his head.**

“Taylor has been my best friend forever, I should go to her party even if that means I can’t go to Adam’s party,” said Johnny. “I better call him.”

“Hello, Adam?” said Johnny. “I’m sorry, but I can’t come to your party on Saturday. Can we go swimming together another day?”

“Sure Johnny! We can go another time,” responded Adam.

“I like the way you thought through that decision, and apologized to Adam,” said Johnny’s mom as they left the house to go shopping.

"I am going to give you some money for a present," said Johnny's mom as she handed him a $10 bill.

"Wow, a lizard sticker book! Taylor loves lizards" thought Johnny. "But the soccer ball is really cool too. Taylor likes to play soccer."

***The price of the sticker book is $10, and the price of the soccer ball is $10. And I only have $10 to spend*. Thought Johnny.**

"Hmmm.... What shall I do?" asked Johnny

LIZARDS
$10
$10

“Well, if you get the ball, you won’t have enough money for the sticker book.” said his mom

“And if I get the book, I won’t have enough money for the ball,” finished Johnny.

“That’s right,” his mom replied.

“If I get the ball, we could play together,” thought Johnny, “If I get her the stickers, she will use them all up and have nothing left to play with.”

LIZARDS

"I'm going to get the ball!" decided Johnny.

That Saturday at Taylor's party, Johnny gave the soccer ball to Taylor.

"A soccer ball, I love it. We can all play soccer together now!"

Johnny and his friends were enjoying the new ball when Taylor's dad shouted "Time for ice cream!"

“Do you want some ice cream Johnny?” asked Taylor’s dad.

“Of course!” Johnny said.

“Cookie dough or chocolate mint?” said Taylor’s dad.

Johnny thought hard…

"BOTH!"

Possible topics to review based on this book:

1. What decisions did Johnny have to make in this story?
2. Did he have to think hard about the decisions he made?
3. What did he think about when he made his decisions?
4. What decisions have you made today?
5. Were they easy or hard decisions to make?
6. What did you think about when you made your decisions?

Economic Ideas:

In this book Johnny had to make a lot of decisions and most of them involved a tradeoff. Tradeoffs occur when you give something up when you make a decision to do something. Economists often use the term "opportunity cost" to measure what you have given up. Often this alternative is measured monetarily, but it does not have to be. Opportunity costs can also be measured in terms of time or other resources.

For example, Johnny decides to go to Taylor's birthday party. The opportunity cost of this choice is going to Adam's birthday. It is also possible to measure Johnny's opportunity cost with time. If the party takes three hours, then the opportunity cost of going to the party is three hours. Similarly, Johnny spends $10 on a soccer ball for Taylor. The opportunity cost of the soccer ball is the $10 he has given up in order to have the ball.

Characters

- Johnny: John Maynard Keynes (1883-1946):
- John was one of the first macroeconomists to formalize arguments encouraging government intervention in the economy. He suggested that currency deflation could boost exports, and public spending could create jobs. John's policies were taken seriously post World War I and were formalized as Keynesian economics.
- Taylor: Harriet Taylor Mill (1807-1858):
- Taylor published little of her own work during her lifetime (this was common for women during this time period unfortunately). She did, however, read and comment on much of the material produced by John Stuart Mill. Mill is famous for his contributions to economic freedom, utilitarian regulation, women's rights, and environmental protection. He claimed that Taylor was a valuable contributor to his work.
- Adam: Adam Smith (1723-1790):
- Adam is considered the "father of modern economics" for his insights presented in the *Wealth of Nations.* He argued that rational self-interest and market competition leads to socially optimal outcomes. He called this process "the invisible hand". Adam can be credited for laying the groundwork for many economics concepts, including supply and demand, marginal analysis, and modern capitalism.

Made in the USA
San Bernardino, CA
26 March 2018